I0487148

Table of Contents

Introduction

Face it; you can't do everything yourself.

While it may seem like common sense, it's not always so easy for new entrepreneurs to acknowledge. They tell themselves that they'll save money if they just do it all themselves.

Perhaps it's the control freak in us who wants to stay in charge of every aspect of our business, or the frugal shopper who wants to save money by just working on projects ourselves.

Regardless of how hard we may try to convince ourselves not to outsource, the bottom line is that delegating important tasks to qualified professionals is simply the fastest way to grow your business and skyrocket your income.

There's another reason why outsourcing is important: when you try to do it all, you're taking 2 big risks. The first is that some tasks and projects won't be done as well as they well as they could be if you had more time, or the necessary training. This could lead to distributing inferior products or low-quality content that won't help move the needle.

The second risk, and it's a big one, is that you'll simply burn out and not be able to stay on top of your market.

No matter how many skills are in your arsenal, or how many years of experience you have, there are **always** tasks that can (and should) be done by seasoned professionals. As the old saying goes, *just because you can do it yourself doesn't mean you should.*

With an outsourced team, you can get the help you need to grow your business faster than ever before, and without worrying about human resources and employment taxes.

Better yet, if you stick with hiring professionals who are

experts in their field, you won't even have to train anyone to complete the tasks you assign to them because they'll already be experienced and ready to take on all that you have to offer.

Outsourcing is the smart way of doing business, building an established presence in your industry quickly and developing a life-long brand that stands out and apart in your niche.

Connecting to seasoned professionals gives you the leg up, allowing you to compete, head on, with some of the biggest names in your niche.

In other words, it levels out the playing field.

In this book, I'll:

- Show you how hiring experienced virtual assistants can help you dominate the market and grow your business quickly. This goes beyond the time you'll save.

- Provide some quick-start tips to help you start using virtual assistants the right way. This information will help you avoid the common pitfalls, ensuring your team stays focused.

- Explain the anatomy of an effective job description (and tell you where to post jobs) so that you're finding the best people for your team. Your job ad or description is one of the most important parts of your outsourcing strategy because it needs to be positioned as beacon that attracts the right candidates – the people who will help your business stand out.

- Walk you through how to qualify the virtual assistants you hire to minimize your risks.

- Show you exactly what should be in a virtual assistant contract to protect your business.

- Outline powerful team-building strategies for working with virtual assistants so you can skyrocket your progress quickly.

By the time you've finished reading this report, you'll be ready to get out there and build your power-house team of professional virtual assistants who will help you get to where you need to be.

Let's get started!

Market Domination

So, you already know that hiring the right team of virtual assistants can help you take your business to the next level of success.

In fact, there's no easier way to expand into new markets and test out new product ideas than with a team of virtual assistants at your disposal.   And if you want to **dominate your industry**, then hiring seasoned professionals will help you do this in a way that might not be possible if you try to go it alone.

How Outsourcing Can Help You Grow Your Business

Virtual Assistants can help you maximize your productivity by allowing you to focus on growing your business. You're the one who needs to go out and attract new business. You're the face of your brand and the voice and mastermind behind the product launches.

That's a huge job in itself! And if you also consider the many different tasks often required in maintaining a stand-out brand, you'll likely find yourself quickly running out of time. Then your business will suffer because you're far too busy trying to micro-manage all the small stuff that you just don't have time left over for what matters.

In other words, if you're bogged down in daily tasks and administration, you won't have time to effectively build your business on a **strong foundation**.

Outsourcing is, for many entrepreneurs, their secret weapon. It allows them the opportunity to expand into new markets they may not be experienced with, and to design, build and product extraordinary content, products, apps and merchandise that they could never create without a team of experts.

Recap:

Outsourcing will help you:

- Expand your services and products
- Automate your systems
- Reach new segments of the market
- Get the benefit of other people's experiences
- Give your customers something new

Need some simple examples?

A freelance writer might be able to make your company blog a must-read for people in your industry or niche by producing pillar content that positions you as an authority and thought-leader.

A skilled marketer could transform your social media strategy and help you fine-tune your campaigns to reach a new audience. Instead of you having to spend weeks learning Facebook ads, hire an experienced campaign manager to launch your marketing campaign for you in a matter of minutes.

Using virtual assistants simply gives you a *ready-made team* to work with that requires little to no training. The people you hire can offer you new perspectives and put their skills to work for you and quite often, they'll be able to help you come up with new ideas and ways of doing things you never even thought of!

In the next chapter, we'll talk about some quick-start strategies so you know how to create a professional team that are focused on helping you build your business.

Quick-Start Strategies

If you've never hired a virtual assistant before, you're probably wondering how they'll fit into your business, or how best to utilize the skills they bring to the table so you're maximizing their value.

That's an important consideration, and it might not be so easy to figure out where to best fill the gaps of your business because you may not even recognize what those gaps are!

In this chapter, I'll explain how to integrate virtual assistants into your system, and give you a step-by-step guide to getting started.

Okay, So Where Can You Use Virtual Assistants?

Virtual Assistants can be beneficial to almost **any part of your business**, regardless of your niche or industry.

For example, you can hire:

- Seasoned writers and authority bloggers.
- Creative web designers.
- Skilled graphic designers.
- Expert marketers and copywriters.
- Freelance accountants and bookkeepers.
- Freelance admin and virtual assistants.
- Coders, programmers and app developers.
- And the list goes on.

How to Integrate Virtual Assistants into Your Business

When you're deciding which virtual assistants to hire, you'll want to start by analyzing your business and then deciding what **key areas** need attention. That way you can hire professionals to work within your existing business system rather than trying to create positions for virtual assistants.

Sounds like common sense?

You might be surprised to discover just how many entrepreneur's hire virtual assistants without a game plan in place. They end up with a team of professionals who are ready to help their business grow, yet no real direction is given.

Don't hire first and then figure it out later.

Start with a solid (and detailed) business plan that outlines where you need help the most, what takes up too much of your time, and how you can tap into the skillset of others to broaden your outreach. Then, fill those spots with seasoned professionals.

Never Outsourced Before?

If you're just starting out, create a framework that outlines your entire business structure as it exists today – as well as where you want it to be in the future.

Example:

Start with the type of products you plan to create including things like blog content, video training, reports, or perhaps an app. Then, move on to focus on how you plan to market your business, what your overall objectives are and where you hope to be in a year from now.

Laying the groundwork for your business is a critical step before you should begin to hire virtual assistants. By knowing what your end-goals are, and how you hope to shape your business, you'll be able to figure out the best way to integrate virtual assistants into your business and what tasks you should be delegating.

Here are some questions to ask yourself:

- What is the most important task(s) that needs attention?
- What task(s) do I not enjoy doing?
- What task(s) do I struggle to do myself, or always find myself falling behind on?
- What tasks are outside of my own skillset?
- How does hiring someone who has a specific skillset help my business grow?

Your focus needs to be on **identifying the most important tasks** that keep your business afloat, or that would help your business get to the next level. Then, determine whether you are capable (and willing) to do the task yourself, or if you are better off seeking the assistance of a seasoned virtual assistant.

This isn't always so easy, especially if you tend to want to do everything yourself! You'll need to take a step back and analyze your business goals carefully.

For example, you might be great with developing a marketing strategy but you lack the design or writing skills to bring a campaign to life. That's when you'd hire a virtual assistant to fill that gap. You may work together on certain tasks, or you may hand over the reins to the entire project – it'll depend on your objective and skillset.

The key is to know **exactly where your business will benefit** from virtual assistants before you even begin seeking them out. Don't rush off to hire a team of professionals without knowing how you'll effectively utilize them so that you're able to put their skills to use and not waste your time and money.

Every virtual assistant you hire should be assigned a specific task (or series of tasks) that help move your business forward in some way.

Tips on Budgeting

Budgeting for virtual assistants means being willing to invest in your business while being reasonable with your expectations.

It may be helpful to shop around and get an idea of the going rates so you know what to expect. And keep in mind that you get what you pay for!

A word of caution: if you hire virtual assistants from sites where the quotes are low, the quality may be as low as the quote. A lot of the writers working for content mills, for example, don't speak English as a first language, so expect to pay more for professional-grade content you can be proud to publish.

Here's how to figure out a reasonable budget before hiring your team of professionals:

1. Decide what your **top virtual assistant priority** is.
2. Look at your **budget** and figure out how much you can afford to spend.
3. Post the job, being **clear** about your spending parameters.

It may take some trial and error to figure out how much you'll need to spend to create your team, but take your time with this! You should focus on filling one position at a time, rather than hiring your entire team in one week.

Your Step-by-Step Guide to Getting Started

To end the chapter, let's run through a quick, step-by-step process for getting started with virtual assistants:

1. Review your needs and decide which tasks you're going to outsource. Remember, your focus should be on gaining access to skills you and your team don't have.

2. Create a budget to pay for your virtual assistants.

3. Write accurate job descriptions. (More about that later.)

4. Post your job descriptions.

5. Evaluate virtual assistants and make offers.

In the next chapter, we'll get into how to write a stand-out job description.

Anatomy of a Stand-Out Job Description

The quest to hire the right virtual assistant for a task starts with a stand-out job description. If your job description is vague or unclear, you may end up attracting the wrong people.

In this chapter, we'll talk about how to write a clear job description, as well as where to post your jobs for maximum exposure.

Tips for Writing a Great Job Description

Your job description should be specific and very direct. You want to attract the best virtual assistants to your company by providing them with all the essential information they need to make an informed decision as to whether they're qualified to handle the tasks you plan to assign.

Here are the critical components of a clear job description that will attract the right attention:

- A compelling headline – something that will make a virtual assistant stop and read your offer. Your headline should include WHO your ideal candidate is.

- A clear description of the work you want done, along with date ranges / time frames, if applicable.

- A list of qualifications. For example, you might want only virtual assistants who speak English as a native language and have at least 2 years of virtual assistant experience.

- A range for compensation, including whether milestones are paid out as tasks are completed or at the end of a project.

- Whether the job is an ongoing one or short-term.

You want the people who read your description to be excited to work for you, but more importantly, to only apply if they can meet your needs. The interviewing process can take some time so the clearer your job description is, the easier it will be to attract qualified professionals who can get the job done.

Where to Post Your Jobs

There are lots of places to post jobs online. Some are more geared toward low-paying jobs, while others are more likely to be places where you'll find experienced virtual assistants. Let's look at some of them and I'll give you a brief description.

- Guru is a well-respected freelancing site with thousands of qualified professionals looking for both short and long-term projects in various fields.

- LinkedIn is a social media site that's ideal for finding virtual assistants and employees in

IT/marketing/writing/design and programming fields.

- Freelancer is a very popular with thousands of virtual assistants looking for jobs in countless markets.

- Upwork is another respected freelancing site and one of my top recommended spots if you're looking for seasoned professionals.

Of course, you can also ask friends and social media contacts for recommendations or do a search for virtual assistants in your area if you want to meet in person.

Once you've posted a job listing and received some quotes, it's time to evaluate the virtual assistants who've contacted you. That's what we'll talk about in the next chapter.

Qualifying Virtual Assistants

There are a lot of virtual assistants to choose from so how do you know which ones to hire?

How to Evaluate Virtual Assistants

It's essential to qualify virtual assistants before you entrust them with any work. Fortunately, this isn't hard to do. Here are the steps you can take to make sure the people you hire are good at what they do.

1. Request samples of their completed work. Any qualified virtual assistant should have a portfolio of samples they're willing to share. The samples should be relevant to what you're asking them to do – if you're hiring someone to write blog posts, they should have sample blog posts.

2. Interview them in person or on Zoom. One of the biggest risks is that a virtual assistant will present themselves as being fluent in English when they're not. Having an in-person or Skype interview will allow you to evaluate them. If they can't speak coherently, they're not going to be able to write coherently, either.

3. Give them a test job. If someone doesn't have samples to give you, you may want to ask them to do a test job for you: a sample piece of writing or a sample design. You should plan to pay them for their work, but it's a good way to get a feeling for what they can do.

4. Google them. This might seem like an obvious step, but I'm amazed when people skip it. If someone's made a habit of plagiarizing work or skipping out with a deposit, there's a good chance their previous victims have written about it online. You owe it to yourself to check.

Don't overlook these important steps. It's worth the time and effort to do you homework and you'll save yourself a lot of aggravation down the line.

How to Minimize Your Risk

The other part of qualifying virtual assistants is minimizing your risks. You can do that by taking a few steps to protect yourself.

1. Get every virtual assistant to sign a written contract that spells out their duties as well as what and how you'll pay them for each completed task or project.

2. Have every virtual assistant sign a non-disclosure agreement (referred to as an NDA) that makes it clear that you own the completed work and they are not allowed to talk about what they do for you. (This can be a clause in the main contract.)

3. Set up milestone goals and payments. You should never pay a virtual assistant up front unless you have worked with them before and are sure they can deliver as promised.

   Instead, create milestone payments that align with project delivery. You should be prepared to make a partial payment up front, but every subsequent payment should be tied to a deliverable.

4. Check for plagiarism. When you hire freelance writers, it's a must to check for plagiarism. You can use sites like Grammarly or Copyscape to do it.

If you do find that work has been plagiarized, you are within your rights to go back and ask them to rewrite the content until it passes a plagiarism check. Never deliver your final payment until you are satisfied with the content.

Coming up next, I'll walk you through the basics of creating a virtual assistant contract.

Creating Contracts

In this chapter, we'll review why contracts are necessary, what you should include in your contracts, and where you can find boilerplate contracts online.

Why You Need a Written Contract

Written contracts are necessary because they ensure that all parties know what's expected of them. They lay out:

- The scope of the work
- Delivery dates and milestones
- Payments and bonuses

It's a good idea to include a non-disclosure clause in your contract, although some employers choose to make that a separate document. That's up to you.

What to Include in Your Virtual Assistant Contracts

Your freelancing contracts must be specific. After all, the contract is the document that you'll use to resolve any disputes about the work completed or the payment for that work.

Here are the items you should include in your contracts:

- The names of the parties and the scope of your relationship
- The work that falls under the contract
- Delivery dates and milestones
- Deposits and retainers, if applicable
- Payment amounts and dates
- A termination clause
- A non-disclosure clause

Including these items will protect both you and the virtual assistant. You may find that some experienced virtual assistants have a contract they ask clients to sign. If that's the case, make sure to read it carefully and have your lawyer review it before you sign.

Where to Find Contracts Online

You don't necessarily need to hire a lawyer to create a virtual assistant contract. If you have the money to hire one, you can, but there are lots of resources online.

Here are a few that I recommend:

- Jotform
- Hloom
- SquareUp
- TemplateLAB

Keep in mind that these are templates. You should feel free to eliminate clauses that don't apply to you or add new clauses as necessary.

Final Words

Thank you for reading *Boss Up & Outsource*. I hope you've found the information here to be useful and that you're ready to start building your virtual assistant team!

To recap, the things you need to do to build your team are:

- Identify the work and projects that are suitable for outsourcing and determine where you need the most help.

- Write a job description that's clear and compelling, making sure to spell out the qualifications necessary for the job.

- Accept quotes and qualify the virtual assistants who respond, making sure to ask for samples, check references, conduct a Zoom interview, and conduct due diligence before choosing your team.

- Create contracts for every virtual assistant that outline important terms including: privacy, milestones, payments, and termination methods.

- Ask the virtual assistant to sign a non-disclosure agreement.

- Provide your team of virtual assistants with the communication, tools, and accountability measures to deliver excellent work.

Good luck building your team of virtual assistants!

www.ingramcontent.com/pod-product-compliance
Lightning Source LLC
Chambersburg PA
CBHW051419170526
45165CB00004BA/1881